Jazz Improvisation

Filling in the Gaps

by Glen Quarrie

ISBN: 1545406200

ISBN-13: 978-1545406205

To Richard Mollek, Norman O'Harra, Scott Ruhe, Howard Willaman and Dave Drummond, the five public school band directors who helped a small-town kid from Ligonier, Pennsylvania get his start in music. School music programs can change lives.

CONTENTS

ACKNOWLEDGEMENTS

Many of the insights, tips and exercises contained in this book are my own and others were picked up along the way from many associates and teachers. Thanks to both those known to me and unremembered who contributed to this work.

Teach Your Brain to Improvise Jazz

Effective improvisation happens almost entirely in the subconscious mind. Great improvisers are not thinking "OK, here's an E7#5 chord. I'm going to play the B# and resolve it up to the C# of the AMaj7 chord." Well, maybe they are a little, but mostly they are playing by ear. A truly effective improviser's subconscious mind creates melodies using programming that has been acquired by focused practicing. Knowledge of chord reading and analysis is of great value, but the purpose of those things and of practicing any number of improvisation techniques should be to train the subconscious mind, providing it with the tools that it needs to create spontaneously "by ear."

This short, easy to read book is designed to help students of improvisation to quickly and efficiently acquire the basic skills that all successful improvisers possess. It is not intended to teach you how to read chord symbols, learn licks or determine what scale to play over a D7#11 chord. That book has been written a hundred times.

The first thing you may notice about this book is that it contains no written musical examples. Instead, the focus is on presenting efficient, productive exercises and developing an understanding of the true nature of the improvisation process that will help to shorten and expedite your journey to becoming a jazz master. It will help you to cut to the chase, to understand what you need to do in order to quickly reach your goals and will teach you how to take maximum advantage of your current abilities.

Whether you are a beginner or a very advanced student, the simple exercises you will learn from reading this book will help you to feed your subconscious mind, addressing your weaknesses and teaching you to focus on the essentials. These exercises won't require you to be organized or to know a lot of harmonic theory. They don't take a lot of effort, nor do they necessarily require daily repetition.

Yet, with application over time, they will yield excellent results. You can even practice some of these techniques, with great benefit, without getting out your instrument. You can do them while riding on a bus, cooking, walking to class etc.

How to Use This Book

Identify your weaknesses and pick some exercises that will help you to strengthen your deficiencies. Practice them whenever you have time.

If there are sections of this book that get a little too technical for you, ignore them for now. Come back to them when you have a little more background. You don't have to do all of the exercises in this book. Think of it as a cafeteria, where you take what you think will nourish you and then come back for lunch again tomorrow.

What's My Problem?

Successful improvisation requires mastery of three fundamental skills. They are *harmonic sense*, *real time composition* and *instrument-specific hearing*. These are like the three legs of a stool. If one leg is weak, the stool will topple. Likewise, your improvisation will only be successful if you are strong in all three areas.

Each of the exercises included here will focus on developing one of the three fundamental skills. Most of them will also provide some crossover benefit, helping to improve the other skills to a lesser degree. Knowing your shortfalls will help you to focus on those exercises that will shore up your weakest areas. Try a few exercises from each chapter and concentrate on the ones that are the most challenging.

Harmonic Sense

Harmonic sense is typically the least developed of the three skills among players of monophonic instruments. Monophonic instruments are those that can only play one note at a time. This includes singers. If you are not sure what your shortcomings are, focus on the exercises in this section initially.

Harmonic sense is the ability to hear a harmony or a sequence of chords and to intuitively understand which notes will sound consonant (pleasing) in that context. It also includes the ability to hear how one note will lead logically to the next as the chords change. This is called voice leading.

Lots of budding improvisers have plenty of cool licks (phrases) to play. Knowing when to play them is the tricky thing. This is dependent on having a strong harmonic sense. In order to develop your harmonic sense, *practice with accompaniment as much as possible!* Play-along tracks, accompaniment generating apps and recording devices can be valuable tools to provide accompaniment for your practicing. Use them!

Maximize Your Harmonic Awareness

When improvising, approach a tune from a macro, not a micro perspective. Know the form of the tune (AABA, ABAC, AABC, etc.) Your intuition for the whole form of a tune will keep you from getting lost and give shape and logic to your improvisations. It gives you a framework to fill in with the minutia of the specific chords later on. When listening to jazz, see if you can identify and follow along with the form of the tune.

When performing, as the ensemble plays the tune's exposition (the composed melody), listen carefully to the bass line and to the chord progression to form a general impression of the shape of the tune. Do the same while any prior soloists play.

Exercise: Playing Along with Random Stuff

Tune in a radio station, navigate to an internet music provider, or put your portable music player on shuffle. Play along with whatever tune comes up. Play simple things and listen intently to how your notes interact with the accompaniment, both when the harmonies are stagnant and as the chords change.

I prefer to play along with music that features vocalists, because the keys tend to be more varied. Also, vocal accompaniments usually define the harmonies more clearly than those on instrumental jazz tracks. If straight ahead jazz, bebop, hard bop, west coast jazz, New Orleans jazz or any related jazz styles are your thing, think Frank Sinatra or the great American song book initially, as you search for play along material. Their chord progressions are fundamentally very similar.

When playing along with recordings, make sure that you adjust your tuning, as necessary, to compensate for differences in pitch caused by variations in playback speed. Playing in tune will help your successes to be more apparent.

Be sure to focus on the interaction between the notes you play and the harmonies on the recording. Listen for consonances (good notes), dissonances (bad notes) and voice leading (forward moving melodies) in your improvisation as the chords change. Stop playing periodically and listen intently to the harmonic progression, including the bass part. Don't worry about taking away anything specific. Don't labor over this. Just do it regularly. You are feeding your subconscious mind, and it will pay you back later!

A great way to accomplish much of the same thing, without spending any extra practice time or tiring your embouchure is to sing, rather than to play along. You can sing or hum out loud or silently to yourself, although singing out loud forces you to commit to a pitch and lets you really hear the consequences. I do this constantly, while riding in cars, in restaurants (silently) and to music on television commercials. Any time you hear music is an opportunity to sing along and develop your harmonic sense.

Exercise: Saturation

Select or create a play along track for a fairly simple jazz tune. Improvise over it using all of the techniques that you know and also entirely by ear. Play many, many choruses of that tune. Use accompaniment programs or apps to change tempos and feels, and to break the tune into smaller sections when possible.

Work on the same tune over the course of several days or weeks. Once you become tired of that tune, pick another and work with it to exhaustion. Learn the heads (composed melodies) at the same time, so you can add these tunes to your repertoire.

Developing an intuition for the chord progressions of a number of simple tunes will develop your intuition for the typical basic jazz chord progressions contained within them, such as 2-5-1 progressions, turnarounds, cycles etc. Having knowledge of a few simple tunes and the basic chord progressions within them will cover a huge amount of ground. You will be amazed how easy it is to hear more complicated tunes, once you learn to intuitively hear and navigate a few simple ones with their fundamental chord progressions, even if you don't have the knowledge to analyze those progressions.

Most jazz tunes change keys frequently within the tune, as often as every two measures, or even more frequently. Navigating these modulations (key changes) is often a greater harmonic challenge than handling the short, familiar chord progressions. One important "key" to hearing modulations is to spend lots of time playing by ear with accompaniment.

When you have a strong sense for basic jazz chord progressions and your instrument specific ear training is in place you will at times feel the desire to play a note that is outside of the key in which you have been playing. This is a modulation (key change.) If at that moment, you feel as if you are on shaky ground, proceed by playing more simply and with smaller intervals, such as whole steps and half steps. This will help you to get a sense of the new key.

Playing the bass line on your instrument (always with accompaniment) is a good way to solidify the timing and sound of the small basic chord progressions and key changes of a tune in your mind.

Don't worry about learning these tunes in multiple keys. The harmonic intuition that you develop will translate to all keys. The greater benefit to your harmonic sense will come from learning a variety of tunes.

Voice Leading, Play It Forward

Most jazz chord progressions use sequences of chords that pull us along in a forward direction. The forward tug of the chord progression results from the resolutions of individual notes within the chords, as they move to nearby notes in subsequent chords. When your improvised melody contains these resolutions, it pulls the listener along with you, adding a huge amount of interest and strength to your line. The note choices you make when resolving one note to the next, as the chords change, is called voice leading.

Exercise: Guide Tones

Learn to intuitively hear and incorporate strong voice leading into your melodies by practicing guide tones. With accompaniment (as always) play the third or seventh of any chord. As the chord changes, move to a nearby chord tone (root, third, fifth or seventh) of the subsequent chord. You will hear the tension in the first chord release as you resolve these guide tones to the next chord.

Also practice resolving any altered tones, such as b9, #9, b5, #5 and sus4 to a nearby chord tone in the subsequent chord (root, 3rd, 5th or 7th.) Doing this on any tune at any time during your practice will yield great results over time.

Paleontology, Know the Bones

Use the bass line and the composed melody to your advantage. Together, they are an easy to learn, encapsulated version of the chord progression. Listening to the bass player specifically and being aware of the melody as you solo will keep you focused on the feel of the chord progression, allowing you to hear the modulations and the best voice leading more automatically. This can also help you to incorporate some very specific voice leading into your improvisation, in the form of notes taken directly from the melody. What could be stronger than to incorporate the best voice leading from the composed melody into your solo?

Keeping in mind the composed melody as you play will also help you to construct a solo that is stylistically appropriate and will help your solos on various tunes to differ from one another, thereby keeping your improvisations fresh.

Exercise: Harmonic Transcription

Don't panic. This is the one and only exercise in this book that absolutely requires some harmonic analysis skills, and it is entirely optional. You can become a great improviser without ever transcribing or analyzing a single chord progression, yet this can help open up your ears, so save this exercise for a time when you are ready. It is very efficient, because like many of the other exercises in this book, it can be accomplished without getting out your instrument.

When listening to any music at any time, listen for the bass part. Use your knowledge of music theory to figure out its function. For instance, you may determine that the tune starts on a 1 chord, then goes to a 2-5-1 chord progression. Sing or play along as needed to figure out the notes and function of the bass line.

As you become more skilled at recognizing bass lines, try to determine the quality (major, minor, dominant etc.) of each chord. Listen to see if the third of each chord is major or minor by singing or playing the major and minor third above the chord's root, in order to better hear which third is consonant. Of course, this requires you to be able to recognize the sound of a major and minor third. Start by singing the bass note, which is almost always the root of the chord, and sing up from there the first three notes of a major scale. If the third note sounds consonant (good), the chord is major. If not, drop the third note down a half step (the smallest interval) in order to hear the minor third.

Once you are able to hear thirds fairly easily, determine if the chords' sevenths are major or minor in the same way. On most minor chords the sevenths will be minor. Listening for sevenths will help you to determine which of the chords with major thirds are major seventh chords and which ones are dominant seventh chords. To hear the quality of the chords' sevenths, sing the bass note, then the notes a half step and a whole step below (the major and minor sevenths), to determine which is consonant. When you are really good, listen for alterations, such as b5 and #5 and to pick out diminished and augmented chords, also b9, sus4 and b5 chords.

You don't need to understand or be able to transcribe a chord progression to have an intuition for it and to successfully improvise on it, but when you are ready, this level of listening will help you to advance your subconscious programming and will pay you back during your improvisation.

Harmonic Ambiguity in the Rhythm Section

Sometimes you may find yourself improvising on a tune, feeling like you just can't make the chord changes. Nothing seems to resolve. You aren't able to accurately describe the chord changes with your improvised melodies. Jazz is a team sport, and to succeed, you've got to know which sport you are playing. Your interaction with the rhythm section will be very different, depending on the style of jazz you are playing and the comping style of your keyboard player, guitarist and other chord-playing instruments. Your improvisation should reflect the comping style.

The type of the harmonic support you get from the rhythm section will vary greatly. As you perform, be aware of your rhythm section's penchant for deviating from the standard or agreed upon chord changes (if for example you are using chord charts.) Your ear is always the final word. Whether or not you are able to recognize how the rhythm section is varying the chords, use your harmonic sense to guide your soloing.

Keyboard, guitar and other chordal instrument players can give you a very clear harmonic platform on which to build your solo, a spare accompaniment that barely describes the chords or perhaps something in between. An extreme example of harmonic ambiguity would be playing your monophonic instrument in a trio with just a drummer and a bass player.

The bottom line is that, an inexperienced player may feel a little lost playing with an ambiguous rhythm section. Knowledge, however, is power. When the rhythm section doesn't clearly outline the chord changes, you have great freedom to superimpose your vision on the tune. There are fewer wrong notes. In the case of the bass trio, there are almost no wrong notes.

In a harmonically ambiguous situation, you can either play outside the changes and be super hip, or use your improvised melody to accurately describe the harmonies as you feel they should be. You have the freedom to play inside the changes until you mess up, at which point you are playing outside and accidentally being extra cool!

Great creative freedom comes from harmonic ambiguity in jazz. A side effect is that this abundance of choice can blur the lines between great and mediocre jazz musicians. The truth is that all great jazz musicians play only so-so at times and most mediocre improvisers play great at times. Use your awareness of ambiguity in the rhythm section to play with authority and confidence as you strive to be one of the greats. You will arrive at your goal sooner and, in the mind of your audience, you will sound great more of the time.

Instrument Specific Hearing

Instrument specific hearing is the ability to play by ear an imagined melody on your instrument, in real time, without having practiced it in its finished form. If you have perfect pitch, feel free to skip this section. However, if you are like the vast majority of the world's great improvisers, and don't have perfect pitch, read on.

In order to develop your ability to translate melodies that you imagine into actual fingerings and note choices, it is important to compartmentalize a little bit. First, be sure that the melody you imagine is clearly formed, rather than a vague impression. If a melody is not clearly defined in your mind, it won't come out as you play.

Exercise: Sing Along with Random Music

To practice committing to a melody, slowly sing out loud with accompaniment. Be decisive. Commit to the notes, whether they are good or bad choices.

When you know what you want to play, use your whole tool kit to find the notes on your instrument. Instrument specific hearing has three attributes, relative pitch, absolute pitch and temporary pitch memory.

Relative Pitch

Relative pitch refers to your ability to find a subsequent note by gaging its interval (distance) up or down from the note you have just played.

The good news is that most jazz melodies consist of small intervals. Half steps and whole steps tend to predominate, followed by minor and major thirds, with larger intervals occurring less frequently. The larger the interval, the less it tends to be incorporated. The smaller the interval, the easier it is to hear and find on your instrument.

Yes, you can occasionally use your solfeggio skills to find the next note, but you generally won't have the time to think "Sounds like the first two notes of Somewhere Over the Rainbow," or "That's the 5th of a D7 chord."

Exercise: Playing Along with Random Stuff - Part 2

Listen to random recordings. Try to pick out and play pieces of some of the melodies that you hear, both composed and improvised.

Exercise: Practice In 12 Keys

Without written music, practice melodies, scales, arpeggios, scale patterns or jazz licks in 12 keys. This material can change each time you practice or you can repeat it over course of days or weeks. As you practice, listen carefully to the transitions from note to note and feel them happening under your fingers or with your trombone slide etc. In short, really experience it and let your subconscious mind learn the pitch relationships between the notes.

Start with simple things. The goal is not to memorize licks by brute force, rather to gradually develop the means to find any melody that you may imagine on your instrument.

It is OK to use written music initially, as long as you are listening carefully. Ultimately, however, you will need to practice these things without music. Use your knowledge of key signatures, intervals and any necessary means to succeed. Listen carefully for mistakes and

14

correct them as you go. As you improve, let your ear guide you more and your analysis less.

Except on string instruments the intervals feel different in each key. Therefore, to develop your sense of relative pitch across your whole instrument, you'll need to do what all excellent instrumentalists do, practice in all 12 keys, listening and feeling intensely as you proceed. Again, start by practicing very simple melodies or patterns, always in 12 keys.

Training your instrument specific hearing is a gradual process. Careful, attentive, quality practice will yield quicker results than hurried, inaccurate practice. You will see results over the course of weeks, not days, so be patient while you use these exercises to hone both your ear and your instrumental technique.

Absolute Pitch

Although it is unlikely that you will acquire perfect pitch, you can definitely improve your ability to find notes based, not on their relationships to one another, but on their actual pitch. Once again, train your subconscious. Always listen carefully to the pitch of each note as you play it. Be aware of the feeling of that note's fingering, trombone slide position, or what have you.

Exercise: Pitch Matching

It may help to play some pitch matching games. Have someone play a random note and try to match it on your instrument, feeling it before you guess. Don't use solfeggio to determine the interval from the last note played. Just hear the pitch, try to feel the fingering that the pitch suggests, and guess.

Alternatively, have a friend play a short sequence of notes or a melody. Try to pick out those notes on your instrument. Focus and try to find the notes on your first attempt.

Don't be frustrated when you fail. Absolute pitch is just one tool that your subconscious mind uses to find the notes on your instrument. As you refine all of the tools of pitch recognition, your results will improve, and you will succeed more and more at easily playing the notes, which you imagine.

Temporary Pitch Memory

Use your short-term pitch memory as you improvise. As you play your solo, be aware of and remember what you have just played. When you want to return to a pitch you recently played, you will know exactly where it is on your instrument. This is especially useful when playing larger, harder to hear intervals. So, add some interest to your improvisation by using your temporary pitch memory to feel confident playing larger intervals.

Melodic Sense

We learn the jazz language, including typical phrasing, licks, tone, inflection, rhythm and timing by listening to great jazz musicians perform. Listen to jazz a lot, when riding the bus , riding in a car, eating, exercising or just for pure pleasure. Focus on one style or artist at times and listen across a broad spectrum at other times.

Exercise: Focused Listening

Examine one artist's playing by editing and placing just his or her solos from a single album or project onto a compiled recording, eliminating the heads (composed melodies) and other musicians' solos. Listening to one musician's solos back to back many times will help you to get that person's "sound" into your ear. You may be amazed to hear the soloist repeat his or herself verbatim many times over the course of an album, playing go-to licks multiple times on different tunes. Likewise, you will discover some of the soloist's bag of tricks. You may want to borrow some of them, whether they are cool licks, typical inflections or phrasing, or any number of other compositional devices.

Exercise: Assimilation

Learn a short fragment of a solo, just a few notes, which you can pick out by ear. Try to play this "lick" along with the recording. See if you can intuitively find other places to play it on the same recording. Use your analytical skills and your ear to practice it in several or all 12 keys.

Focus on Rhythm and Sound

There are many ways to draw in your audience that don't require you to be a brilliant composer or to have an extraordinary ear. Relax when you play, and focus on matching the ensemble's timing as exactly as you can. This works best when you rely on your own internal sense of pulse, making subtle adjustments to match the rhythm section as needed. Don't let the excitement of the moment cause you to rush ahead. Having good time makes you sound professional.

Use repeated rhythms at times and purposely vary them at others to avoid long strings of eighth notes and to strengthen your melodies. The stronger your rhythms, the less anyone will care about variety and intricacy in your melodic lines.

The same holds true for having a great tone and varying your sound to add interest. This may involve bending pitches, altissimo playing, using false fingerings, growling, using mutes and any effects and inflections that add a vocal quality to your playing. We are programmed to respond to the human voice, so play vocally.

Motives

Motives are short, strong melodies or melodic or rhythmic ideas that are not tied to any specific chord progression. They serve as reference points or handles that will help you to organize your soloing and to give you confidence while at the same time adding strong melodic content in your solos.

Motives can be more versatile than licks, which apply to specific harmonic situations, such as your favorite 2-5 lick or your go-to turnaround. I don't actually have many licks memorized, except by accident, never having had the patience to memorize licks and force them into tunes as I practice. This is not to say that I don't play idiomatically or use common jazz expressions. If you work to develop your melodic vocabulary through careful listening and have a well-trained harmonic sense and solid instrument specific hearing, you will find that you can play idiomatic jazz phrases spontaneously, adapting them easily to your improvisation. The whole process becomes much more fluid.

Exercise: Practice Using Motives

To practice incorporating motives, invent a short, strong melody or rhythm. Use it, or some variant of it in multiple places as often as you can while practicing with play-along material or while playing along with random recordings. Use the motive as the basis for your improvisation, playing it in some form or another, multiple times, during your solo while transposing it, altering some of the notes, stretching or contracting the rhythm etc.

A motive is source material. Any idea that derives from and suggests the original motive can be used in the course of a solo. Invent a motive and work with it for a minute or for several minutes during practice, molding and evolving it and then abandon it. Try using two or more motives within the same solo.

Motives can easily contain larger leaps than the small intervals, which are the staples of most jazz improvisation, thereby providing a handle to help you incorporate some interest into your improvisation without the fear of missing notes. Having played a motive once, you have a handle to hold onto, a pitch and interval reference to help find more notes on your instrument as you forge a solo.

Using motives will help you to focus your practice. Incorporating them into your improvisations will engage your audience enabling you to play many tunes during a gig with great variety.

Using Structural Elements in Melodies.

A great improvised melody pulls the listener along. One way to accomplish this is for your melody to have strong structure, independent of the chord progression. Your melody may have a certain geometry based on repetition. For example, you may play three scale tones going down followed by a leap up, repeating this shape several times. Or, you may use the same interval or intervals repeatedly. For example, you may incorporate lots of fourths and half steps into your melody. Any device you use to structure a melody and make it meaningful or beautiful, independent of the chords, will strengthen your improvisation and give your melody forward motion.

Exercise: Practice with Structured Melodies.

Compose a short melody that is not based on any particular chord progression. You may or may not want to base it on some compositional device, such as a pentatonic or whole tone scale, the use of major thirds, or a contour of upward and downward motion. Regardless of how you achieve it, the melody should feel like it has meaning unto itself.

Now play the melody everywhere, whether it fits the chords or not. Play it with various accompaniment tracks, while playing along with random stuff, anytime and anywhere. Try to resolve it when you complete the lick, ultimately making sense of it in the specific harmonic context. Learn it in several or in all 12 keys if you like. Now you're playing outside of the chord changes with purpose.

Ornaments

Learn to use ornaments such as surround tones and appoggiaturas to fix mistakes. If you play an obviously bad note, make it the first note of an ornament, thus changing its function from a landing point to a point of tension that will then be resolved.

Exercise: Ornamentation

When practicing with accompaniment compose a little melody that incorporates surround tones. Before you play a chord tone, add the notes just above and below it (or below and above.) The surround tones will serve to emphasize the chord tone. The two surround tones can either be from the corresponding scale or they can be the nearest half steps above and below the target note (chromatic neighbor tones.)

You can use this device to add interest to your solos or to bail yourself out when you accidentally land on a note that is one tone removed from the note you intended. Just make the bad note the first note of a surround tone.

Use appoggiaturas in the same way. An appoggiatura is a note that is outside of the harmony, which occurs on a downbeat and is then resolved down a whole or half step to a chord tone. When you land on a bad note, resolve it down a whole step or half step. You are often just one step away from a good note.

Exercise: Practice Phrase Endings.

Compose or copy from recordings some short phrases that feel very final. With accompaniment, work hard to incorporate some of these ideas at the conclusion of various spontaneously improvised phrases.

7 Goes to 8, 6 Goes to 5, 4 Goes to 3, 2 Goes to 1

When playing melodies, regardless of the chords in question, very often the 7th note in the key likes to resolve to the 8th, the 6th to the 5th, 4th to the 3rd and the 2nd to the 1st. This is more or less independent of the actual chords being played, as long as you remain in one key. Experiment with this while playing with accompaniment on a medium or slow tempo tune that stays in the same key for a period of time.

Set Yourself Free

It's very liberating to have a balanced mastery of the three skill sets. Removing barriers is the surest way to help develop your own style!

In a Nutshell

The four most productive things you can do to rapidly improve as an improviser are as follows.

1) Play and sing along with accompaniment to develop your harmonic sense.

2) Practice licks, scales, arpeggios, etc. in all 12 keys to develop your instrument specific hearing and technique.

3) Listen to jazz regularly and pick out bits of your favorite jazz solos and licks to play by ear to develop your melodic sense.

4) Continue to study jazz theory and harmony to provide a basis for your ear training.

Maximize Your Current Abilities

Adjust to Your Mistakes

If you play a wrong note, change the rest of your phrase to make sense of the mistake. Make something of whatever the unexpected direction in melody suggests. This is more of an attitude than a practice technique, so adopt a "never say die" attitude.

Alternatively, if you play a phrase that doesn't resolve well, make your next phrase the same or similar to it, but with a better resolution. This will legitimize the preceding subpar phrase as a setup for the final one.

The chromatic Scale

Practice the chromatic scale regularly, and use it to fix mistakes. If you hit a wrong note, play half steps until you land on a good one. The chromatic scale is consonant in all situations until you come to rest. It is also boring and nondescript, due to its symmetry (all half steps), so don't overdo it.

Use the chromatic scale to connect notes that are far apart. If you really want to play a distant note next as part of your solo line, but you aren't sure where that note is on your instrument, connect it to the note you are currently playing with a glissando (rapid chromatic scale.)

In other words, play all of the half steps in between as you transition from one note to the next. This will help you to hear the interval. Just stop the glissando when you hear that you have arrived at your target note.

Although you will hear professional players occasionally using this technique, you will be wise to save it for times when you need a bailout. If overused, excessive glissandos can sound amateurish. However, in the right context, glissandos can be musically satisfying with the added benefit of helping you to incorporate some interesting large intervals into your soloing.

Strategize

Don't play too many notes too fast. Focus on content. It's OK to leave some empty space in a solo, while you listen and get your bearings. Space can be musically satisfying.

The corollary to this is: Do play way too many notes, really fast. This can dazzle your audience and get them in your court when you don't have a clue what is going on, especially if your melody has a strong structure that is independent of the harmonies. Play fearlessly "outside of the chord changes" as you try to regain your bearings and search for a strong resolution. Look confident. After all, you "meant to do that!"

Play to your audience, not to the other, potentially more hip members of the band. Ask yourself, "What does the audience need?" Notice that I didn't say "What do they *want*?" It's OK to be sophisticated, just not self-indulgent.

A typical improvised line consists of several ideas strung together. These ideas come from your musical vocabulary, which develops over a lifetime of playing music and practicing improvisation. Except for the final idea in a string, none of the ideas needs to resolve. Instead, one idea can flow logically into and suggest the next.

Your line will be judged by how you resolve the last idea. Every mistake, clam and left turn that you play prior to the final resolution will be deemed "genius, awesome outside playing and truly unique," if you nail the final resolution.

Try to play two or three ideas, resolving the last one. If you fail to resolve the last idea successfully, keep going with one more idea and resolve that one, etc. until you nail it. Then pause in celebration and start again. If, at the end of your solo, you succeed in resolving a phrase nicely and you have another two measures to go, resist the urge to play a final flourish. It likely won't be musically satisfying, and you run the risk of not being able to resolve it successfully before you run out of solo space. Just take a two-measure long bow!

Know Your Own Playing

Periodically, record yourself while playing with accompaniment, whether it is with a backing track or in a live playing situation. Listen to your improvisations. What do you want to work on? Is it your tone or possibly your time? Are your phrases too long? Do you panic? Do you stick to what you already know too much or maybe take too many chances? Do you have any annoying habits or use a certain cliché too often?

There is no magic formula for great improvisation, but knowing your weaknesses and strengths will help you to focus when playing live and when practicing. Listening from the audience's perspective is a completely different experience. You will definitely be surprised at what you hear on your recording.

Make It Work Now

Streamline Your Path to Success

Very often a young star achieves notoriety because he or she has specialized, putting most of his or her energy into becoming a great jazz saxophonist, perfecting the Hummel trumpet concerto or playing blues guitar. That musician may or may not also be a great reader, doubler or be able to play well in other genres. What people notice and appreciate is the advanced skills that the musician is demonstrating here and now.

The point is, if you want to be noticed, specialize first, then branch out as you mature.

Let's take this to the next level. You can be an amazing improviser today, if you pick one simple tune and break it down and work on it very hard. During the process, you will find things that work in the context of that tune. You will most likely end up repeating material from one take to the next, but when you perform that tune for a fresh audience, you will leave them with the impression that you are a really good jazz musician.

The point is that you don't need to have a perfect ear or a lifetime of experience to play jazz well. When performing publicly, play what you know, and skip the rest. As much as possible play tunes with which you are familiar. Use motives, rhythm, inflections and any other handles that allow you to create a reasonable improvisation, while accurately describing the tune's chord progression. Use what you *can* do as a basis for acquiring new skills.

I have managed to succeed at and improve my improvisation by following an 80/20 rule. Within a solo, I usually try to play 80% of stuff that I'm reasonably sure will succeed and 20% of stuff that is risky, experimenting with things that I have only tried in the practice room, or that come to mind at the moment. In critical situations, I usually play it safer than 80/20.

Don't Take on the Big Dog

Sometimes playing jazz can feel like a contest. If you are sharing the band stand with a great player, don't try to beat him at his own game. If you are forced to solo directly after the big dog, start your solo in a contrasting style then take it anywhere that is musically satisfying, forgetting what came before. If the big dog's solo is going to follow yours and likely blow the audience away with flash, make this an embarrassment by playing with great sensitivity. Stay within your means, and do what you do best. Don't let your audience compare apples to apples. Just make your best music. Now who's the big dog?

Look the Part

Conduct yourself as if you are already an accomplished pro. Be humble, confident and not overly apologetic. Be enthusiastic and demonstrate a willingness to go the extra mile without seeming naive. Be appreciative of your musical betters, but don't relegate yourself to a lower tier by constantly praising them or comparing yourself to them in a negative way. Connect with your musical peers on a human level, as much as possible. People tend to hire their friends first and the best players second.

Dress appropriately. Be clean. Don't smell. Be early. Be organized. Be reliable. Don't back out of a gig in order to take a better one. Be honest. Be fair and up front with the money. Meet lots of musicians and music industry people and stay in touch with them. Constantly work on your skills. Enjoy making music, and have fun!

Glen Quarrie studied saxophone and jazz studies at Carnegie Mellon University and Indiana University. He taught saxophone, improvisation and jazz studies at Carnegie Mellon University from 1987-2007. He has toured and played saxophones, flutes, clarinets and oboes with as he puts it "anyone who used to be someone" (and a lot who still are.)

He is currently a freelance woodwinds guy for musical theater pit orchestras and, in between, plays one-nighters in the jazz clubs and regularly with the All Star Super Band and the Little Lake Stompers in Milwaukee.

Glen tips his hat to the world's greatest soul band, Johnny Angel and the Halos.

CPSIA information can be obtained
at www.ICGtesting.com
Printed in the USA
LVHW081621210119
604670LV00036B/1717/P